☆ CHEER SPIRIT ☆

SHOW YOUR SPIRIT

Cheerleading Basics
You Need to Know

by Rebecca Rissman

Consultant:
Tara L. Wieland
Owner and Head Coach
Michigan Storm Cheer and Dance
Midland, Michigan

CAPSTONE PRESS
a capstone imprint

Snap Books are published by Capstone Press,
1710 Roe Crest Drive, North Mankato, Minnesota 56003
www.capstonepub.com

Library of Congress Cataloging in Publication Data
Rissman, Rebecca.
  Show your spirit : cheerleading basics you need to know / Rebecca Rissman.
     pages cm. — (Cheer Spirit)
  Includes webography.
  Includes bibliographical references and index.
  ISBN 978-1-4914-5214-1 (library binding)
  ISBN 978-1-4914-5222-6 (eBook PDF)
  1. Cheerleading—Juvenile literature. 2. Cheers—Juvenile literature. I. Title.
  LB3635.R58 2016
  791.6′4—dc23
                        2015009410

Editorial Credits
Abby Colich, editor; Heidi Thompson, designer; Tracy Cummins, media researcher;
Katy LaVigne, production specialist

Photo Credits
AP Photo: Robert E. Klein, 13; Capstone Press: Karon Dubke, 10-11, 28, 29; Getty Images: Dick Durrance II/
National Geographic, 9, Hunter Martin, 20-21, Joshua C. Cruey/Orlando Sentinel/MCT, 16, Lambert, 8,
Tony Anderson, 25; iStockphoto: Andrew Rich/Rich Vintage Photography, 18-19, Steve Debenport, Cover;
Newscom: Megan Maloy Image Source, 24; Shutterstock: Aspen Photo, 5, 12, 26, Richard Paul Kane, 15,
Robert Adrian Hillman, Design Element, surachet khamsuk, Design Element, tmcphotos, 23, zsooofija,
Design Element; Thinkstock: nicolagoddard, 30; Courtesy of University of Minnesota Archives, University
of Minnesota - Twin Cities: 5, 6

Printed in the United States of America in North Mankato, Minnesota.
052015   008823CGF15

TABLE OF CONTENTS

"GET FIRED UP!"

Hey, girl! It's game day and the home team needs you. It's time to cheer, cheer, cheer!

Modern cheerleading is very different from its historic roots. Today's cheerleaders put on an awesome show. They shout catchy chants and cheers. Advanced squads even wow the crowds with acrobatics, stunts, and gymnastics.

Cheerleading is a sport that is growing rapidly in the United States. More than 3 million people are members of cheerleading squads. The best cheerleaders show their skills at national competitions. They can even earn college scholarships.

Is Cheerleading a Sport?

You may have heard people arguing about whether cheerleading is a sport. Try this on for size. A 100-pound (45-kilogram) girl burns 272 calories in an hour of cheerleading. That's the same amount she'd burn playing an hour of competitive volleyball.

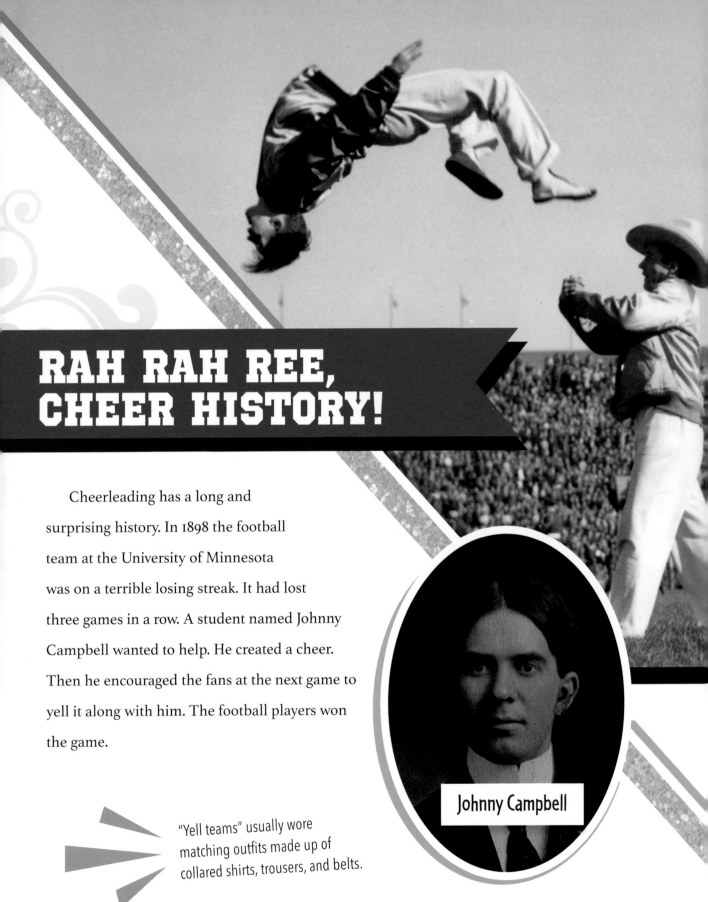

RAH RAH REE, CHEER HISTORY!

Cheerleading has a long and surprising history. In 1898 the football team at the University of Minnesota was on a terrible losing streak. It had lost three games in a row. A student named Johnny Campbell wanted to help. He created a cheer. Then he encouraged the fans at the next game to yell it along with him. The football players won the game.

Johnny Campbell

"Yell teams" usually wore matching outfits made up of collared shirts, trousers, and belts.

After this exciting win, Campbell knew he was on to something big. Along with five other male students, he formed a "yell team." The "yell team" at the University of Minnesota was the first ever cheerleading squad. The "yell team" came to all the games to cheer with the crowd. This seemed to boost the athletes' spirits. Soon "yell teams" and "yell squads" formed at schools all over the nation. Cheerleading was born.

The first cheerleading squads were all male. In the 1920s a few eager women started to join. In the 1940s, when many men left to fight in World War II, cheerleading became a mostly female sport.

Around the same time, cheerleaders began using props. These included megaphones, signs, and pom-poms. Early pom-poms were made of delicate tissue paper. As cheerleading evolved, pom-poms became more durable.

By the 1960s cheerleading began to look like the modern sport of today. Squads were still mostly female, but some men participated. In the 1970s cheerleading became more athletic. Squads began performing amazing stunts and skills.

Two U.S. presidents, Dwight Eisenhower and Franklin Roosevelt, were members of their schools' cheer teams.

All-star cheerleading competitions started in the 1980s. These are contests for advanced squads. Around this time, the role for male cheerleaders began to change. They acted as bases and spotters during stunts—lifting, throwing, and catching female cheerleaders. Male cheerleaders also began to tumble and cheer once again. Today cheerleading is an exciting show of both school spirit and athletic ability.

female cheerleaders, 1955

University of Alabama cheerleaders, 1975

Cheerleading is a great way to have fun, stay fit, and make friends. Many things go into creating a cheer routine. The four main parts are cheering and chanting, motions, tumbling, and stunts. These all add up to one goal—getting the crowd to cheer for the home team!

CHEERING AND CHANTING

Cheers are long and are usually linked with motions. Chants are shorter and are often repeated by the crowd.

MOTIONS

Motions are crisp body positions. Put together in a sequence, these motions become routines.

TUMBLING

Advanced squads use tumbling to wow the crowds. Handstands, flips, and handsprings are all examples of tumbling.

STUNTS

Very advanced teams use stunts to show off their skills. Pyramids and lifts are common stunts.

CHEER HERE, CHEER THERE, CHEER EVERYWHERE!

The most popular sport for cheerleading is football. Cheerleaders for football cheer outdoors in many different weather conditions. Football cheerleaders need to be extra loud. They often cheer in front of long bleachers full of excited fans.

Cheerleaders also cheer at basketball games. These squads are often smaller than they are for football. Basketball cheerleaders cheer on the sidelines while the game is in play. During time-outs and halftime, they may cheer in center court.

Some squads cheer at wrestling matches. Wrestling cheerleaders sit near the wrestlers. They pound the mat, encouraging the wrestlers and energizing the crowd.

Some cheerleaders cheer along with the school's pep band. A pep band is a small school band that plays at games, rallies, and other school events.

Some squads participate in cheerleading competitions. These are contests for different squads to show their best cheers, chants, stunts, and skills. Some competitions are small and local. Others are very big and include squads from around the country or world.

WORK IT!

On game days cheerleaders have many important jobs. Before the game begins, cheerleaders stand on the sidelines and pump up the crowd. Once the action starts, cheerleaders work with the crowd and pep band to inspire the athletes to do their best!

A cheerleader's work isn't done after a game. In fact, it's just beginning. Cheerleaders help boost school spirit all year long. They perform at pep rallies, make banners and posters, and march in community parades. They also strive to be positive role models and good students.

Cheerleaders encourage good sportsmanship. They never encourage booing or negative cheers from the crowd.

B-A-S-I-C LEARN THESE BASICS 1-2-3!

The best cheerleading routines are loud, inspiring, and in sync.
To achieve this, cheerleaders need to become pros at a few basics.
Even the most advanced cheerleaders work hard on these skills.
Learning the basics helps cheerleaders do their best at games,
matches, and competitions.

ALL TOGETHER NOW!

In most cheer routines, all cheerleaders do the same moves at the same time. In order to do this, squads practice in front of mirrors. Coaches make sure that each movement looks the same.

Small differences can make a squad look out of sync. Coaches show squad members how to hold their hands, head, and body in each movement. This is to make sure that each move looks the same.

Moving all together takes practice. The more a squad cheers together, the better it will get at moving together. It is helpful to move to the beat of each cheer. It is also helpful to watch other squad members out of the corner of your eye. This helps each squad member be sure they are moving at the same time.

CHEER TIP! Flex! Make your stationary positions look great by flexing your muscles.

BE LOUD!

Cheerleaders need to be heard. They are often cheering in front of huge crowds. In competitions cheerleaders must make sure the judges can hear and understand them. Cheerleaders at games often have to shout over noise from athletes, fans, and the weather. The following tips help make sure cheers are loud and clear.

★ Clearly pronounce each part of each word. Do this especially for consonant sounds. Some words, such as "fight," "might," and "night," can sound similar if you don't say the first letter clearly.

★ Cheering each word together is another way to make sure fans understand. Cheering to a beat can help squad members cheer together.

★ Look where you cheer! Facing the crowd or judges makes voices sound much louder.

CHEER TIP! Don't scream! Screaming won't make you louder. It will just make you harder to understand.

BE INSPIRING!

Nothing is more exciting than getting a crowd to cheer along at a close game. It takes more than being loud, clear, and enthusiastic. Cheerleaders work hard to make sure every fan in the stands is inspired to clap, shout, and stomp.

MIX IT UP

Changing positions keeps fans interested. Squads may stand in long rows, in small groups, or even in a pyramid. Moving around on the sidelines helps cheerleaders get close to different sections of the stands. Judges also like to see cheerleading squads use the full stage at competitions.

MAKE EYE CONTACT AND SMILE

Cheerleaders should look at the fans while they're cheering. And when in a competition, they should do the same with the judges. Making eye contact is a great way to get people pumped up.

PUT YOUR BEST FOOT FORWARD

Cheerleaders have their work cut out for them. They need to inspire crowds, wow judges, and root for athletes. However, they must also take care of themselves. Cheerleaders need to eat right, stay safe, and wear the right clothing.

FIGHT, FIGHT, FIGHT! AND EAT RIGHT, RIGHT, RIGHT!

Food is fuel. Drinking enough water and eating the right foods give athletes energy and strength. Cheerleaders should avoid foods that will bring energy down.

 Eat these:

whole grains; fresh fruits and vegetables; lean protein, such as almonds, beans, and turkey; low-fat dairy

 Avoid these:

regular soda and diet soda; processed snack foods, such as chips and candy; full-fat dairy

Game Day Sample Menu for a Student Athlete

Breakfast: granola with low-fat yogurt and sliced banana

Snack: ¼ cup of almonds

Lunch: turkey and hummus sandwich on whole wheat bread,
carrot sticks, string cheese, and an orange

Snack: 1 cup of trail mix (raisins, peanuts, dried cranberries,
chocolate chips)

Dinner: chicken breast, steamed broccoli, brown rice,
and fruit salad

23

STAY SAFE! HEY! HEY! STAY SAFE!

Cheerleaders are fit, daring, flexible ... and safe! Great cheerleaders know how important it is to stay safe. Following these safety rules during every practice and game will help prevent injuries:

★ Always listen to your coach.

★ Never practice tumbling on your own.

★ Only practice stunts if you have at least one spotter.

★ Stretch before and after cheering.

★ Wear sunscreen for any outdoor daytime performances.

★ Do not perform any stunt or cheer that causes pain.

★ Drink plenty of water before and after cheering.

★ Never chew gum or suck on hard candy or mints while cheerleading.

★ Make sure your cheerleading area is flat and clear before you start.

CHEER TIP!

Remember to always take off your jewelry. A sharp ring or bracelet could cut you or a teammate.

HEY HO, HEY HO! DRESS THE BEST FROM HEAD TO TOE!

Cheerleaders have the special task of putting on an athletic show while looking great. The right uniforms help accomplish this. They are comfortable, appropriate for the weather, and show a team's colors.

Cheerleading uniforms are all a bit different, but they usually include similar items. Female cheerleaders usually wear a skirt over bloomers or "spankies." On top they wear a shirt that says their team or school name. It can be a tank top or long sleeved, depending on the sport and the weather. Male cheerleaders usually wear long pants on the bottom, with a tucked in short-sleeved shirt on top.

Both male and female cheerleaders wear shoes made especially for cheerleading. These shoes help them to safely jump without getting hurt.

Most cheerleading leagues have rules about how cheerleaders can wear their hair. They are usually not permitted to wear hair clips. Someone could get cut by a hair clip during a stunt.

Some squads use props such as signs, pom-poms, or megaphones. These will usually belong to the squad. Occasionally cheerleaders are asked to buy their own. Pom-poms are often made from bright, shiny material that matches a school or team colors.

LET'S CHEER!

Now you know what it takes to be a great cheerleader. Try this simple football chant on your own. Start out by memorizing the words. Then try to match the motions to the words. Finally, invite your friends to do it with you. Remember to be in sync, loud, and inspiring!

Words:

Knock 'em down!

Toss 'em around!

Do that defense work!

WORK!

Motions:

Start in Ready Position.

While you say **"Knock 'em"** come to High V Position.

While you say **"down"** come to Low V Position.

While you say **"Toss 'em"** come to Left 5 Position.

When you say **"around"** come to Right 5 Position.

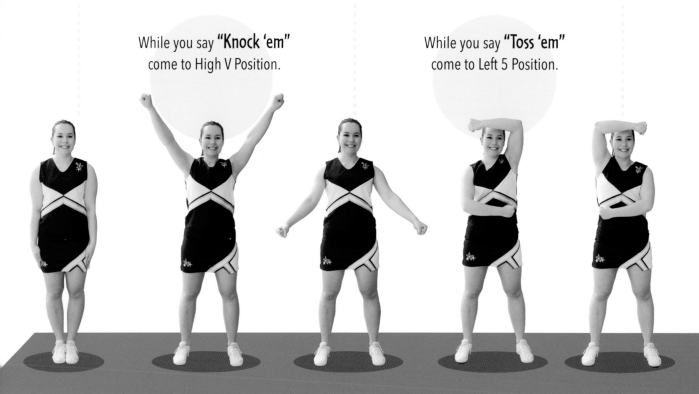

Repeat three times. The more a crowd hears it, the more they will want to cheer along!

When you say **"defense"** come to Daggers Position.

When you say **"WORK"** come to T Position.

When you say **"do that"** come to Ready Position.

When you say **"work"** come to Half T Position.

Return to Ready Position before starting the chant again.

DO YOU HAVE WHAT IT TAKES?

Cheerleading is a big commitment. It takes practice, work, and determination. Cheerleaders need to be good at balancing their different responsibilities. In addition to practice and games, cheerleaders need to make time for homework, family, friends, and down time. They should never sacrifice grades, family, or friends for cheerleading.

Cheerleaders also need to be friendly, kind, and outgoing. They don't just cheer for athletes. They also cheer for one another. Cheerleaders encourage each other to do their best, on and off the field.

Cheerleading is hard work, but it can also be fun. It's a great way to make new friends. It will require you to work your body and mind hard, which will help you feel good about yourself. If you think you have what it takes, grab your pom-poms! Try out for your school or community cheerleading squad, and show your cheer spirit!

READ MORE

Hunt, Sara R. *You've Got Spirit: Cheers, Chants, Tips, and Tricks Every Cheerleader Needs to Know*. Minneapolis: Millbrook Press, 2013.

Webb, Margaret. *Pump It Up Cheerleading*. Sports Starters. New York: Crabtree Publishing, 2012.

Webber, Rebecca. *Varsity's Ultimate Guide to Cheerleading*. New York: Little, Brown, and Company, 2014.

Welsh, Piper. *Cheerleading*. Fun Sports for Fitness. Vero Beach, Fl.: Rourke Educational Media, 2013.

INTERNET SITES

FactHound offers a safe, fun way to find Internet sites related to this book. All of the sites on FactHound have been researched by our staff.

Here's all you do:

Visit *www.facthound.com*

Type in this code: 9781491452141

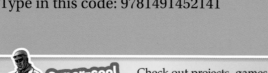

Super-cool stuff! Check out projects, games and lots more at www.capstonekids.com

INDEX